# Zoo Map

**David Tunkin**

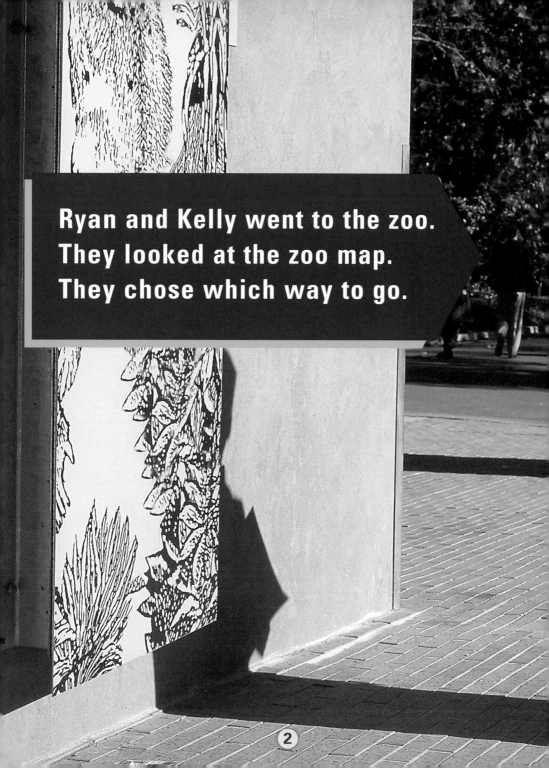

Ryan and Kelly went to the zoo.
They looked at the zoo map.
They chose which way to go.

3

Ryan and Kelly went to see the lions.
What did they see on the way?

To
Lions

Seals

To
Kangaroos

Tigers

Lions

Ryan and Kelly went to see the kangaroos. What did they see on the way?

Seals

To Kangaroos

Alligators

Kangaroos

To Bears

Flamingoes

Hippos

⑦

To
Bears

**Ryan and Kelly went to see the bears.
What did they see on the way?**

Elephants

Zoo Exit

Bears

Vultures

Zebras

9

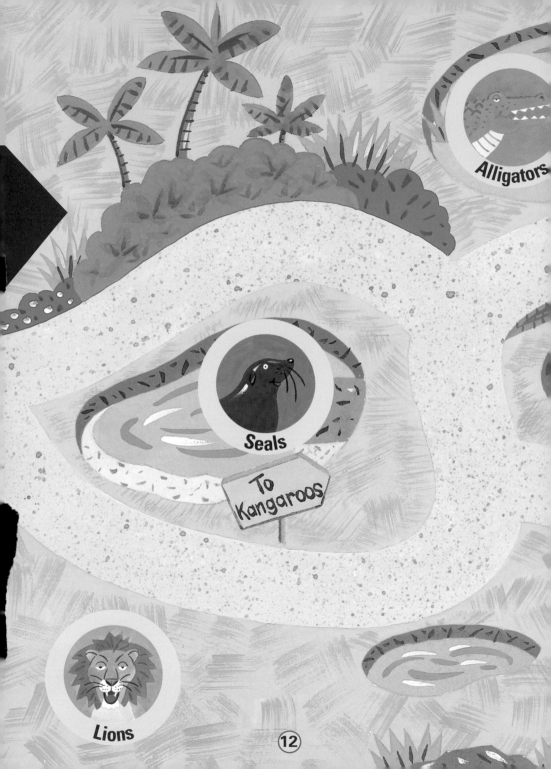

Alligators

Seals

To Kangaroos

Lions

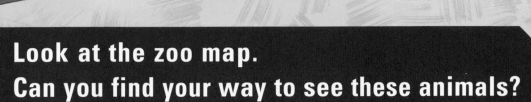

## Look at the zoo map.
## Can you find your way to see these animals?

## How would you get there?

Which animals do you like to see at the zoo?
Open the page to see the zoo map.

Kangaroos

To Bears

Flamingoes

Hippos

# Picture Glossary

**Alligators**

**Bears**

**Elephants**

**Flamingoes**

**Hippos**

**Kangaroos**

**Lions**

**Monkeys**

**Seals**

**Tigers**

**Vultures**

**Zebras**

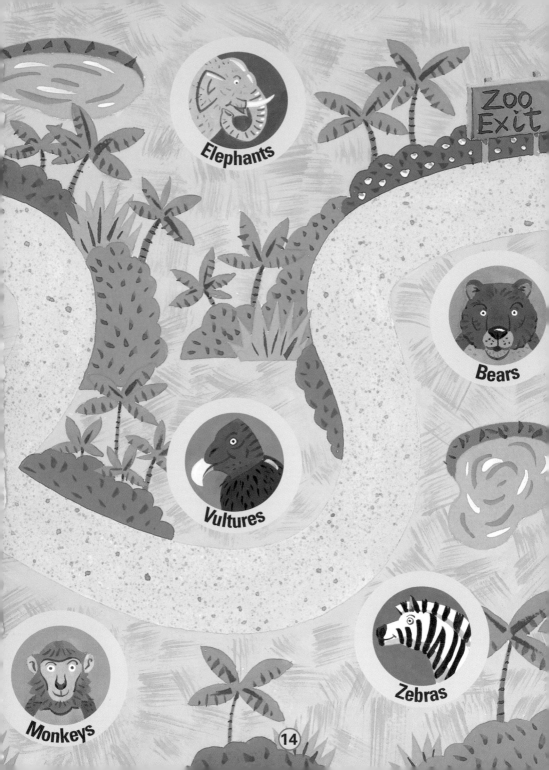